THE NATURE KIDS GUIDE TO
ARCTIC FOXES

DAVID ANDERSON

LP Media Inc. Publishing
Text copyright © 2026 by LP Media Inc.
All rights reserved.

For information address LP Media Inc. Publishing,
30012 Variolite St NW, Princeton MN 55371
www.lpmedia.org

Publication Data

Arctic Foxes
The Nature Kid's Guide to Arctic Foxes — First edition.

Summary: "Learn all about Arctic Foxes, the Nature Kid Way"
— Provided by publisher.

ISBN: 979-8-89818-122-2

[1. Arctic Foxes – Non-Fiction] I. Title.

Title: The Nature Kid's Guide to Arctic Foxes

CONTENTS

FROZEN TUNDRA

The Arctic tundra stays frozen for about nine months each year. Arctic foxes can survive temperatures as cold as -58 degrees Fahrenheit.

Yip! A small fox trots across the snow. Its white fur blends with the ice.

Arctic foxes live in one of the coldest places on Earth. They make their homes on frozen **tundra**. This icy land has snow for most of the year.

The tundra has very few trees. Strong winds blow across the flat land. Winter is long and very cold. Summer is short and cool.

Arctic foxes dig dens in hillsides. These underground homes keep them safe from harsh weather. The dens stay warmer than the frozen ground above. Some fox families use the same den for many years.

ARCTIC ATLAS

Crunch! An arctic fox walks on frozen ground. Its paws grip the ice.

Arctic foxes live all around the North Pole. You can find them living in Alaska. They live in Canada too. They also live in the coldest parts of Russia and Greenland.

Arctic foxes live in Iceland. They roam across the northern parts of Norway, Sweden, and Finland.

These foxes do not move south. They stay in the far north all year long. They like the cold and snow.

Arctic foxes live farther north than any other land predator on Earth today!

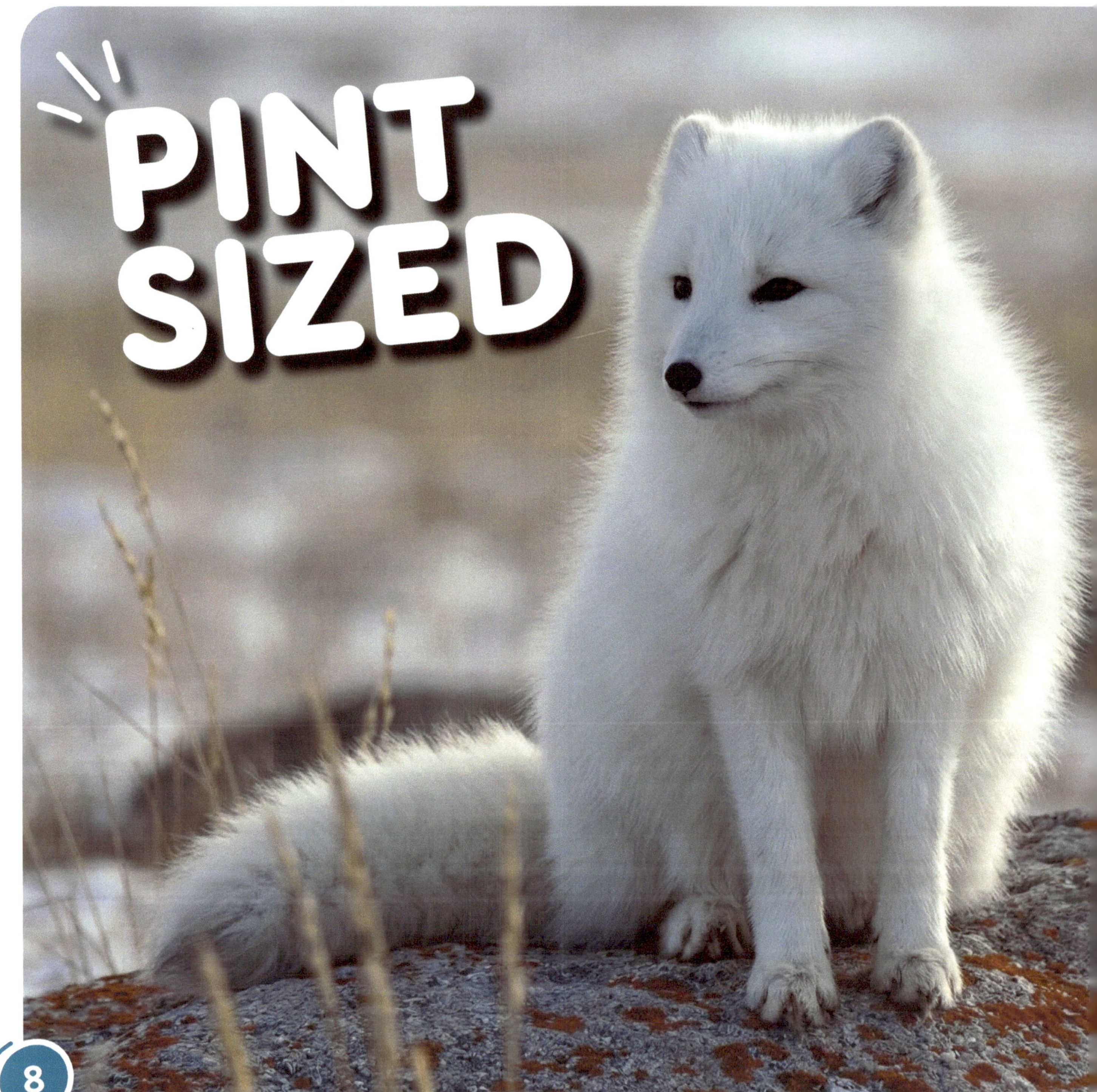
PINT
SIZED

Squeak! A tiny arctic fox sits on a rock. It looks small in the snow.

Arctic foxes are small. They weigh 6 to 10 pounds. That is like a house cat.

These foxes stand 10 inches tall. Their bodies are 18 to 27 inches long. Their fluffy tails add 13 more inches.

Arctic foxes are the smallest member of the dog family in the Arctic. Being small helps them stay warm.

Arctic foxes have the warmest fur of any mammal, even warmer than polar bears!

FLUFFY FEATURES

Fluff! An arctic fox shakes its thick coat. Fur covers its whole body.

Arctic foxes have special body parts for cold weather. Their ears are short and round. These small ears lose less heat than big ones.

Thick fur covers their whole body. Even the bottoms of their paws have fur. This keeps their feet warm on ice and snow.

Arctic foxes also have short legs and short snouts. This compact shape holds in body heat. A bushy tail wraps around them like a blanket when they sleep.

SUPER SENSES

Sniff! An arctic fox lifts its nose. It smells something far away.

Arctic foxes have amazing senses. Their hearing is very sharp. They can hear small animals moving under deep snow.

Their noses work well too. Arctic foxes smell food from far away. They can even smell dead animals buried in snow.

Good eyesight helps them spot prey. Their eyes see well in dim winter light.

Arctic foxes can smell a seal's den under three feet of snow!

CLEVER CAMO

Swoosh! An arctic fox blends into the white snow, hiding in plain sight.

Arctic foxes have amazing **camouflage**. Their fur changes color with the seasons. This helps them hide from predators.

In winter, their coats turn white. This white fur matches the snow and ice. Wolves and eagles cannot see them easily.

In summer, the fur turns brown or gray to match rocks and dirt. The color change takes a few weeks each season.

Some arctic foxes stay gray-blue all year. They live near rocky coasts.

HUNGRY HUNTERS

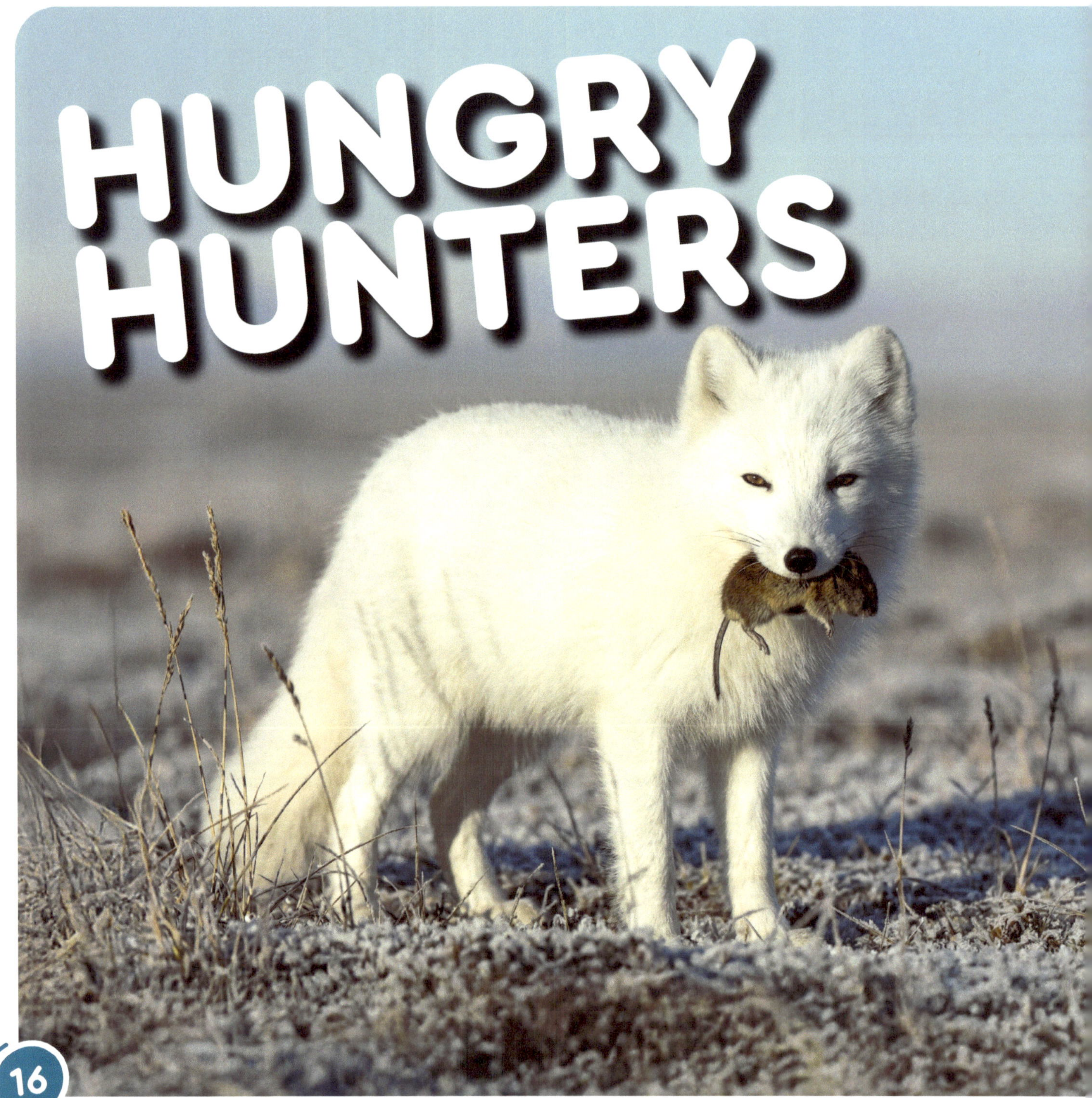

Chomp! An arctic fox catches a lemming and darts away fast.

Arctic foxes eat many kinds of animals. Lemmings are their favorite food. One fox family can eat dozens of lemmings each day.

These foxes hunt birds too. They also eat bird eggs. In summer, they catch fish. They munch on berries too.

Arctic foxes save extra food in summer. They hide it under rocks. They bury it in the ground. This food helps them live through winter when food is **scarce**.

One hungry fox can eat 100 lemmings in a single day!

POUNCE TIME

Pounce! An arctic fox leaps high into the air and dives into the snow.

Arctic foxes have a special way to catch food. They jump high and dive headfirst into snow. This hunting move is often called mousing.

The fox listens for sounds under the snow. When it hears a lemming, it arches its back and gets ready to spring.

Then it leaps up and lands nose-first in the deep snow. Its nose punches through the hard crust, and the fox grabs the lemming with its teeth.

Arctic foxes can pounce through snow up to three feet deep to catch prey.

WATCH OUT

Wolverines also hunt arctic foxes. They can chase foxes through deep snow.

An Arctic Fox spots a Golden Eagle in the sky! The fox must run.

Arctic foxes have many predators. Golden eagles hunt these small foxes from the sky. They swoop down with sharp talons.

Polar bears sometimes catch arctic foxes too. Snowy owls are also a danger, especially for young foxes. Wolves and red foxes will attack when they get the chance.

Young foxes face the most danger. They are small and cannot run fast yet. Predators watch for kits playing near their dens. Mother foxes must always stay alert.

QUICK ESCAPE

22

Snap! An arctic fox hears danger. It darts away fast.

Arctic foxes are quick runners. They can reach speeds of 30 miles per hour. This helps them escape from predators.

These foxes know their home well. They remember where to find safe hiding spots. Rocks and snow drifts make good cover.

Arctic foxes also use their dens to escape. They dive into tunnels when danger comes close.

Arctic fox dens can have more than 100 entrances. Some dens are over 300 years old!

FAST FEET
24

Thump! An arctic fox runs across the tundra, its legs moving fast.

Arctic foxes are built to move. Their legs are short but strong. This helps them stay low to the ground in cold wind.

These foxes trot for many miles each day. They search large areas for food. Some travel over 90 miles in one day!

Arctic foxes can also swim across icy rivers. Their thick fur keeps them warm in the freezing water. They swim to reach new hunting grounds or escape predators.

Arctic foxes have fur on the bottom of their paws. This helps them grip slippery ice.

DAY BY DAY

Rustle! An arctic fox wakes up at dusk. It stretches and gets ready to hunt.

Arctic foxes can be active at any time of day or night. They spend many hours hunting for food. Their white fur helps them sneak up on **prey**.

During the day, arctic foxes often rest in their dens. They curl up tight to stay warm.

At night, arctic foxes come out to explore. They use their sharp ears to hunt for prey under the snow.

Arctic foxes groom their fur often. They lick and nibble their coats to keep them clean and fluffy.

27

FOX FAMILIES

Bark! Two arctic fox kits play near their den. White fur keeps them warm.

Arctic foxes often live in family groups. A mother and father work together to raise their kits. Both parents bring food to the den.

Families stay together through summer. The kits learn to hunt by watching their parents.

Some older kits help care for new babies. They help feed and protect the little ones.

Arctic fox families can have up to 25 kits in one litter. Both parents help feed them.

FINDING MATES

Screech! A male arctic fox calls out. A female fox listens nearby.

Arctic foxes find mates in early spring. Males call out to females with loud sounds. They also leave scent marks on rocks and snow.

A male and female form a pair. They stay together for the breeding season. Some pairs stay together for many years.

After mating, the pair finds a den. They get ready for their kits to arrive.

Male arctic foxes bring food to females during pregnancy, traveling up to 10 miles to find meals.

TINY KITS
DID YOU KNOW?
Arctic fox kits weigh only about two ounces when they are born. That is lighter than a tennis ball.

Squeek! A baby arctic fox peeks out of its den. It sniffs the cold air.

Arctic fox babies are called **kits**. They are born in spring or early summer. A mother can have five to ten kits at once.

Newborn kits are very small and helpless. They are blind and deaf at first. Their fur is dark brown or gray, not white like their parents.

Kits grow fast. Their eyes open after about two weeks. Soon they start to explore outside the den.

By fall, the kits are almost full grown. Their fur turns white for winter.

GROWING UP

Young arctic foxes leave home at about four to six months old.

Growl! A young arctic fox chases its sibling. They tumble and play.

Arctic fox kits grow up quickly. They drink milk from their mother for the first few weeks. Then they start eating meat brought by both parents.

Kits learn skills through play. They chase each other and practice pouncing. This helps them become good hunters.

By late summer, young foxes hunt on their own. They catch bugs and small animals.

By one year old, arctic foxes are adults. They are ready to live on their own.

ARCTIC SURVIVORS

Crunch! An arctic fox walks on frozen snow.

Arctic foxes have amazing ways to survive the cold. Their fur is extra special. It covers every part of their body, even the bottoms of their paws. The scientific name for arctic fox means "rabbit-footed" because of this fluffy fur.

When blizzards hit, they dig into the snow to stay warm. Their bushy tails wrap around their faces like a blanket.

They bury extra meat and eggs in the frozen ground. The Arctic is like a giant freezer! They dig up these snacks when winter food is hard to find.

FINDING FOXES

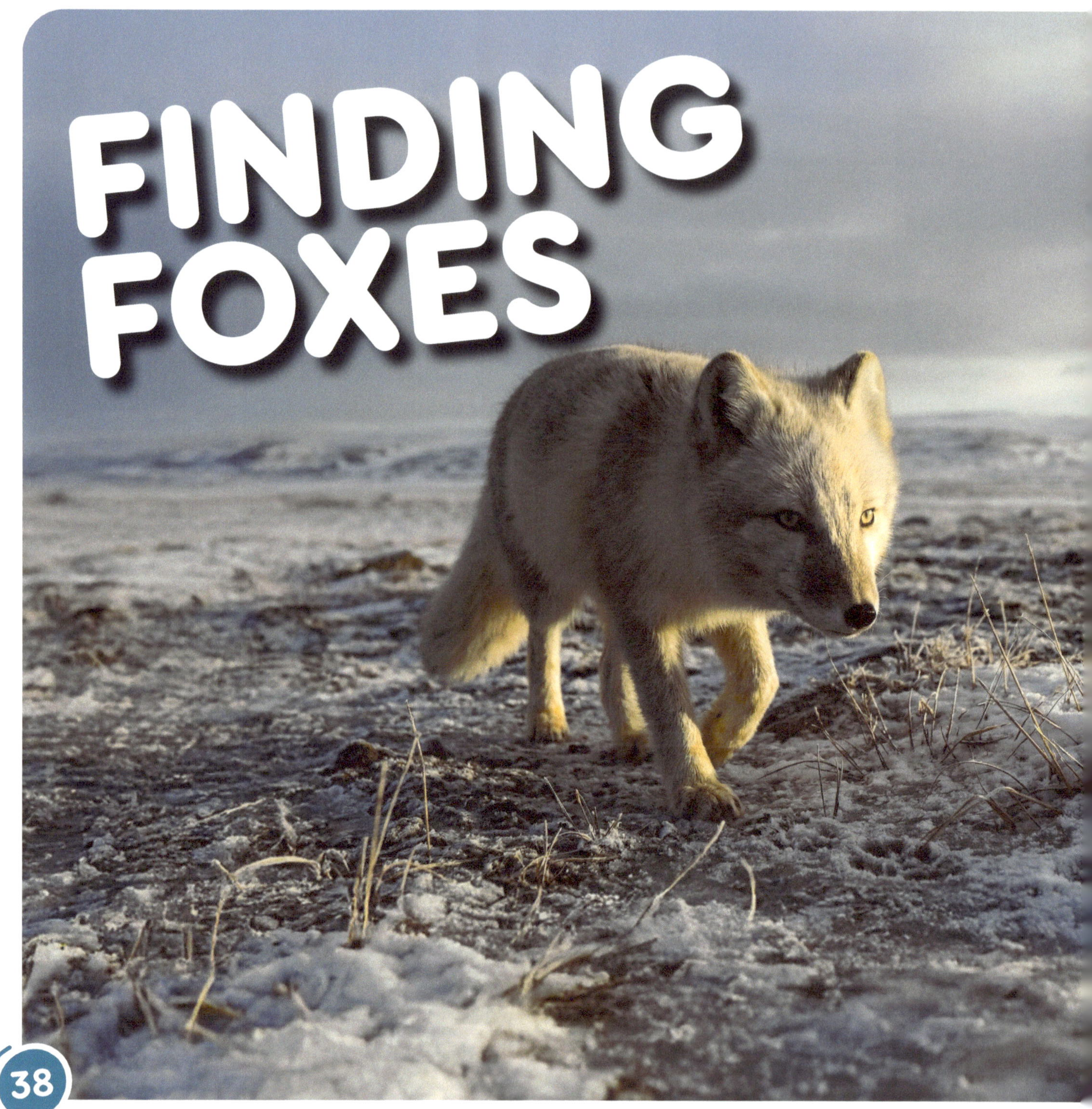

Crunch! An arctic fox walks on frozen ground.

People travel far north to see arctic foxes. They live near the Arctic Circle, which is hard to get to. They are hard to spot in winter.

Wildlife tours take people to see them. Guides know where foxes hunt. Early morning is a good time to look.

Many zoos also have arctic foxes. This is how most kids get to see them without having to travel far north.

Arctic foxes can be seen in Iceland, Canada, Norway, and parts of Alaska.

GLOSSARY

camouflage
Colors or patterns that help an animal hide by blending in with what is around it.

kits
Baby foxes.

scarce
Hard to find or rare.

prey
An animal that is hunted and eaten by other animals.

tundra
A cold, treeless land found in the Arctic. The ground stays frozen most of the year.